At the Sky's Edge

Poems 1991-1996

D0988618

Also by Bei Dao

POETRY

The August Sleepwalker (1990)
translated by Bonnie S. McDougall

Old Snow (1991)
translated by Bonnie S. McDougall
and Chen Maiping

Forms of Distance (1994)
translated by David Hinton

Landscape Over Zero (1996)
translated by David Hinton with Yanbing Chen

Unlock (2000)
translated by Eliot Weinberger and Iona Man-Cheong

SHORT STORIES

Waves (1990)
translated by Bonnie S. McDougall
and Susette Ternent Cooke

ESSAYS

Blue House (Zephyr Press, 2000)
translated by Ted Huters and Fengying Ming

BEI DAO

At the Sky's Edge

Poems 1991-1996

BILINGUAL

TRANSLATED BY David Hinton

Foreword by Michael Palmer

A NEW DIRECTIONS BOOK

Acknowledgments from *Forms of Distance:*
Some of the poems in *Forms of Distance* have appeared in the following periodicals: *Cellar Roots, International Quarterly, Manhattan Review,* and *Sulfur.* The translator wishes to acknowledge the invaluable assistance of Hong-yue Guo, with whom he consulted throughout the translation process, and Yanbing Chen, who vetted the final manuscript.
The publisher would like to thank Norstedts Forlag, Stockholm, for their kind permission to reproduce the Chinese text from the Swedish edition of this work.

Acknowledgments from *Landscape Over Zero:*
Landscape Over Zero was translated by David Hinton with Yanbing Chen. Some of the poems in this book have appeared in the following periodicals: *Conjunctions, Grand Street,* and *The Troubadour.* Translation of this book was supported in part by the Witter Bynner Foundation.

Manufactured in the United States of America
New Directions Books are printed on acid-free paper.
First published as New Directions Paperbook 934 in 2001
Published simultaneously in Canada by Penguin Books Canada Limited

Library of Congress Cataloging-in-Publication Data

Bei Dao, 1949-
    [Poems. English & Chinese. Selections]
    At the sky's edge: poems 1991-1996 / Bei Dao ; translated by David Hinton ;
    foreword by Michael Palmer.
       p. cm.
    Bilingual.
    A New Directions book.
    Includes Index.
    ISBN 0-8112-1495-8 (pbk.)
    1. Bei Dao 1949 – translations into English. I. Hinton, David, 1954- II. Title.
    PL2892.E525 A25 2001
    895.1'152—dc21   2001030838

New Directions Books are published for James Laughlin
by New Directions Publishing Corporation
80 Eighth Avenue, New York, NY 10011

目录　Contents

Foreword

Would that it were possible, right at the outset, to consign the "Misty Poets" rubric to those cultural bureaucrats' file cabinets from which it first emerged. However accurate a rendering of the Chinese (*menglong*), in English it inevitably suggests a stale, neo-romantic impressionism that has nothing to do with the work of Bei Dao or of other poets captured by the term. Nothing to do with the complex interweaving of inner and outer worlds, the private and the public, the personal and the official, the oneiric and the quotidian, the classical and the contemporary. Nothing to do with the act of resistance to cultural orthodoxy their work represents, and nothing to do with their critical deconstruction of the language of power and oppression. Nothing to do with the quest for a radical and responsive subjectivity, a lyric instrument of discovery and disclosure.

It can be a mixed blessing when a poet's work acquires sudden notoriety and immediate historical and political pertinence. Certainly it is fortunate when, due to particular historical and social conditions, poetry is attended to beyond the narrow confines of a strictly literary community. In such circumstances, the territory of its conversation expands dramatically, and poetry can seem to make things happen in ways Mayakovsky briefly thought possible, and Auden notoriously denied. Yet poetry must also always *be* "something happening"—to language, to consciousness, to time and memory. Lacking that dimension, it is no more than verse, cultural décor, reflecting modes of representation and affect already habitual. The temptation of early fame is to abandon the work to a delusional and self-glorifying instrumentality. We saw this happen all too often among the public poets of the sixties and seventies, whose voices grew hollow as they basked in their celebrity status, and their need for immediate response became akin to an addiction. The ironic result was that, instead of critiquing the materialism, prevarications and repression of their cultures, the poetry too often came to seem a pure product of those same cultures, exhibiting the same desires and the same emptiness. The terrible trap of sloganeering is that poetry can end up echoing that very discourse of power and control it sets out to resist.

Anointed as an icon on the Democracy Wall and as the voice of a generation by the events of Tiananmen Square in 1989, and thereby also fated to exile, Bei Dao has followed a path of resistance that abjures overt political rhetoric while simultaneously keeping faith with his passionate belief in social reform and freedom of the creative imagination. Under the guidance of such determinedly resistant poetic intelligences as Mandelstam, Celan and Vallejo, he has continued to develop and deepen his own poetics, even as the conditions of exilic displacement have exacted such enormous tolls on his personal life. In fact it seems to me that it is the very condition of exile that has helped Bei Dao come to more intimate terms with that displacement at the core of all significant, exploratory lyric poetry. I do not mean by this to invoke some hoary, romantic cliché of poetic alienation. Rather, I am speaking of the displacement *into* alternative temporal and spatial organizations that we tend to repress in order to configure or project a more or less linear narrative of everyday life. (Our culture is littered with verse designed to reinforce that same, annealing or consolatory version, as if that were true realism.) The poet disappears—almost disappears—into this deterritorialized, lyric space while becoming, to borrow a term from Pessoa, the *resonateur* of various forces and tones of the mind and the world. What results is a poetry of complex enfoldings and crossings, of sudden juxtapositions and fractures, of pattern in a dance with randomness. It is a perilous negotiation, dependent for its coherence on a depth of attention, of listening, and a commitment to that which is not yet known, rather than to the given.

We are not speaking of "pure poetry," whatever that might be, but of one that is as open to the noise of the world, and to the inhumanity and mendacious bleatings of authority, as it is to the information of dream, the immediacy of memory and the knowledge that arrives with loss. The "I-do-not-believe!" (from his early poem "The Answer") that became a rallying cry for the Democracy Movement continues to resonate through Bei Dao's later poetry. The commitment to a radical reenvisioning of experience, however, has grown progressively bolder and more assured. The conjuring of the uncanny and the indeterminate within the folds of the actual now seems less a literary debt to Surrealism than an existential acknowledgement of continuous passage through different landscapes and codes, the randomness of circumstance brought to a pitch by the poem's intense, echoic compression: "dust of the private/litter of the public." The work, in its rapid transitions, abrupt juxtapositions and frequent recurrence to open syntax evokes the un-speakability of the exile's condition. It offers us, as perhaps poetry most precisely can, the paradox of uncontrollable and/or aleatory forces—of history, memory, dream, the subconscious—being brought to form within the poem. Yet what Bei Dao constructs is a form faithful to the flux itself, to the vortex of experience, and to the constant reconfiguring of time and space within that vortex. It is a poetry of explosive convergences, of submersions and unfixed boundaries, "amid languages." Seeds are sown on marble floors, seasons break loose from their sequence. The subject multiplies, divides, disappears into the "wound of narration." We hear a voice at once out of time and caught in streaming time. The poem projects both the "fire of the venture" and the "ash of the unknown." First, for Bei Dao, the rescue of subjectivity, followed by the deepening knowledge of what that subjectivity can be.

I recently attended a literary festival in Berlin. Bei Dao, Eliot Weinberger, Charles Simic and I were invited to speak on a panel about "Writing from a Distance." We discussed the multiple meanings of nearness and distance in our work and lives, and the far-away-near of writing itself. The following day, Bei Dao left for Rotterdam, after which would come Berlin again, then Vienna, Oslo, Paris, and New York, to be followed by a brief teaching residency in Wisconsin. He travels without a passport.

—Michael Palmer

Forms of Distance

Translated by
David Hinton

岁末

从一年的开始到终结
我走了多年
让岁月弯成了弓
到处是退休者的鞋
私人的尘土
公共的垃圾

这是并不重要的一年
铁锤闲着,而我
向以后的日子借光
瞥见一把白金尺
在铁砧上

YEAR'S END

from the year's beginning to its end
I've walked through countless years
time bending as a bow
shoes of those who've retired scattered
dust of the private
litter of the public

it's been a perfectly normal year
my sledgehammer sits idle, and yet
borrowing the light of the future
I glimpse that metric standard in platinum
here on the anvil

缺席

大风统帅着敌对的旗帜
一声金星喊遍四方
爱与憎咬住了同一个苹果
梯子上的年龄
民族复兴的梦想
英雄高举手臂占据夜空
小丑倒立在镜中的沥青上

我关上假释之门
抗拒那些未来的证人
这是我独享尊严的时刻
冒险的火焰
陌生的灰烬

ABSENT

vast winds commanding hostile flags
Venus fills all four directions with its lone cry
love and hate bit into the same apple
and now it's the age for climbing ladders
it's the pipe-dream of national renaissance
heroes occupying night skies raise their arms high
clowns in a mirror doing handstands on asphalt

I close the door parole proffers
refuse all those witnesses to the future
these moments are mine to savor dignity in solitude
fire of the venture
ash of the unfamiliar

夏日的黄铜

一个谣言的儿子
坐在节育的花环上：
听夏日的黄铜

步伐整齐的士兵
沿着生锈的道路走来：
看夏天的黄铜

树上深深的斧痕
永远迷人的微笑着：
吃夏日的黄铜

BRASS OF A SUMMER'S DAY

lone son born of rumor
sits atop flower wreaths of contraception:
hearing brass of a summer's day

soldiers on the march
come along streets of rust:
watching brass of a summer's day

deep ax cuts on trees
smile fascinated forever:
eating brass of a summer's day

午夜歌手

一首歌
是房顶上奔跑的贼
偷走了六种颜色
并把红色时针
指向四点钟的天堂
四点钟爆炸
在公鸡脑袋里
有四点钟的疯狂

一首歌
是棵保持敌意的树
在边界另一方
它放出诺言
那群吞吃明天的狼

一首歌
是背熟身体的镜子
是记忆之王
是蜡制的舌头们
议论的火光
是神话喂养的花草
是蒸汽火车头
闯进教堂

MIDNIGHT SINGER

a song
is a thief who's fled across rooftops
getting away with six colors
and leaving the red hour-hand
on 4 o'clock heaven
4 o'clock detonates
in the rooster's head
and it's 4 o'clock delirium

a song
is an ever hostile tree
beyond the border
it unleashes that promise
that wolf-pack feeding on tomorrow

a song
is a mirror that knows the body by heart
is the emperor of memory
is the flame spoken by
waxen tongues
is the flower garden nurtured by myth
is a steam locomotive
bursting into the church

一首歌
是一个歌手的死亡
他的死亡之夜
被压成黑色唱片
反复歌唱

广 告

丁香在黎明的丝绸上蹀脚
鸽子在朗读人类之梦
大减价的气候里
我们听见了黄金的雷声

自由步步为营
夜的痛苦被一只猫眼放大
变成了巨型轮胎
婚配的影子紧急转弯

由报纸选举上的新独裁者
在城市的裂缝招手致意
乞求战争的炊烟爬升到太阳的
高度,这是花店开门的时间

a song
is the death of a singer
his death-night
pressed into black records
singing over and over and over

ADVERTISING

lilacs in the silk-cloth of dawn stamp their feet
as doves read the human dream aloud
in this climate of king-size price reductions
we hear the thunder of gold

advancing freedom consolidates its gains step-by-step
a cat's eye dilates night's anguish
until it's a huge tire
shadows of marriage make an emergency turn

a dictator freshly elected by the newspapers
waves warm greetings from a crack through the city
kitchen smoke begging for war rises into solar
heights, now's the time a flower shop opens

多事之秋

深深陷入黑暗的蜡烛
在知识的页岩中寻找标本
鱼贯的文字交尾后
和文明一起沉睡到天明

惯性的轮子，禁欲的雪人
大地棋盘上的残局
已搁置了多年
一个逃避规则的男孩
越过界河去送信
那是诗，或死亡的邀请

AUTUMN WORLD IN TURMOIL

a candle sunk in depths of darkness
hunts for specimens in the shale of knowledge
streaming word-shoals mate
then sleep beside civilization till dawn

inertial wheel, ascetic snowmen
the endgame on chessboard earth's
hung fire for years
a boy escaping regulation
crosses the river-boundary to deliver a letter
that's the poem, or perhaps death's invitation

以外

瓶中的风暴率领着大海前进
码头以外,漂浮的不眠之床上
拥抱的情人接上权力的链条
画框以外,带古典笑容的石膏像
以一日之内的阴影说话
信仰以外,骏马追上了死亡
月亮不停地在黑色事件上盖章
故事以外,一棵塑料树迎风招展
阴郁的粮食是我们生存的借口

BEYOND

a storm in a bottle is leading the sea's advance
beyond the harbor, on a floating bed of sleeplessness
embracing lovers link the chains of power
beyond the picture frame, a plaster figurine's classical smile
takes the shadow within day for speech
beyond conviction, a fast horse catches up with death
and the moon never stops leaving its seal on black events
beyond the story, a plastic tree flutters in the wind
that grain of gloom our pretext for existence

致 T. TRANSTRÖMER

你把一首诗的最后一句
锁在心里——那是你的重心
随钟声摆动的教堂的重心
和无头的天使跳舞时
你保持住了平衡

你的大钢琴立在悬崖上
听众们紧紧抓住它
惊雷轰鸣,琴键疾飞
你回味着夜的列车
怎样追上了未来的黑暗

从蓝房子的车站出发
你冒雨去查看蘑茹
日与月,森林里的信号灯:
七岁的彩虹后面
挤满戴着汽车面具的人

FOR T. TRANSTRÖMER

you take the poem's last line and
lock it center heart———it's your center of gravity
center of gravity in a church swinging among tolling bells
dancing with headless angels
you kept your balance

your grand piano's on clifftops
the audience grabbing it and holding tight
a crash of thunder strikes, a flight of keys
you wonder how that night train
caught up with tomorrow's darkness

leaving your blue train-station house
you brave rain to check mushrooms
sun and moon, forest signal-lights
behind the seven-year-old rainbow
a capacity crowd's wearing automobiles as masks

走 廊

那些啤酒瓶盖
被流动的大街输送到哪儿
那年我逃学,在电影院
在银幕无尽的走廊里
我突然被放大
那一刻是一把轮椅
其余的日子推着我远行——

全世界自由的代理人
把我输入巨型电脑:
一个潜入字典的外来语
一名持不同政见者
或一种与世界的距离

走廊尽头,某些字眼冒烟
被偷走玻璃的窗户
面对的是官僚的冬天

CORRIDOR

all those beer-bottle caps
where were they taken down moving streets
that year I cut class, in movie houses
inside the endless corridor of screens
I suddenly found myself enlarged
that moment was a wheelchair
and the days to come pushed me through distant travels———

the world's agents of freedom
entered me into their giant computer:
an alien voice sneaking into the dictionary
a dissident
perhaps a form of distance from the world

where the corridor ends, various words smolder
and a window robbed of its glass
faces the bureaucratic winter

午后随笔

女侍沉甸甸的乳房
草梅冰激凌

遮阳伞礼貌地照顾我
太阳照顾一只潮虫

醉汉们吹响了空酒瓶
我和烟卷一起走神

警笛,收缩着地平线
限制了我的时间

水龙头干吼的四合院
升起了无为的秋天

AFTERNOON NOTES

huge breasts on a waitress
strawberry ice cream

an umbrella looks after me politely
sunlight looks after a water-bug

drunkards blow on empty wine bottles
my cigarette and I get dreamy

a siren tightens the horizon
hemming in my time

in the courtyard of a dry water-tap's roar
effortless autumn's risen selflessly

剧作家

月亮产后虚弱的早晨
一把椅子在月台上站稳
火车无声地出发
拉锁般展开那秘密的风景
琴声震落了漫天大雪
火光从马厩探头
指示牌被逐个唤醒
岔道分开了黑夜与白昼
终点：一个预订的房间

他打开阳台双重身份的门
把烟雾介绍给晴空
大雨淋湿了那些稻草人

PLAYWRIGHT

in the moon's morning of postpartum convalescence
a chair's stationed on the railway platform
the train's mute departure
zips open that secret landscape
where music thundered down a skyful of snow
and flames in the stables venture forth
direction signs awaken one-by-one
night and day diverging where the routes fork
destination: a room booked ahead

he opens doors of double-identity onto a balcony
and introduces smoke to clear blue skies
those scarecrows drenched after heavy rains

悲 歌

焊接天空的电弧光
象旧日激情
在寻找新的伤口
寻找档案中的暴风雪
风箱里的火星

梦大汗淋漓
象水雷追逐着船只
大海突然干涸了
帐篷林立
我们伤口般醒来

另一种语言的绅士们
穿过难民营

LAMENT

incandescent arc welding the sky
like long-lost passions
searching for new wounds
searching for blizzards amid archives
sparks in the bellows-chamber

dreams drop with sweat
like underwater mines longing for a ship's touch
now the sea's gone suddenly dry
a forest of tents appears
and we wake like wounds

dignitaries speaking some other language
stroll through the refugee camp

苹果与顽石

大海的祈祷仪式
一个坏天气俯下了身

顽石空守五月
抵抗着绿色传染病

四季轮流砍伐着大树
群星在辨认道路

醉汉以他的平衡术
从时间中突围

一颗子弹穿过苹果
生活已被借用

APPLE AND BRUTE STONE

in the prayer ceremony of ocean
a storm bows down

stone watches over May in vain
guarding against that green contagion

as the four seasons take turns axing huge trees
stars try to recognize the road

a drunk using that talent for balance
breaks out from the time-siege

a bullet soars through the apple
life's on loan

空 城

多疑的气候和帆一同起落
死者象影子追随着生者
灵魂和磁化的罗盘
迷失在单行道的中心
白昼的广场,夜的甲板
夜的右翼栖息着灯火
左翼浸入污水中

长发的深渊在追问
海员和它过去的女友们
追问家和触礁的经验
从底版到照片
长发变白,深渊凸现

沉重的星期六
正在驶向一座空城

EMPTY CITY

sails and a climate of suspicion bob up and down together
and the dead trail after the living like shadows
the spirit with its magnetic compass
finds itself lost at the heart of a one-way street
day's town square, night's boat deck
night's right wing perching among the lights
its left founders in open sewers

an abyss of long hair interrogates
the mariner and his long-lost lovers
interrogates impressions of home and ships run aground
from negative to photograph
long hair turns white, the abyss rises into view

a ponderous Saturday
sailing toward the empty city

桥

我调整着录音机的音量
——生存的坡度
旧时代的风范和阳光一起
进入某些细节,闪烁

早晨的撑船人穿越墙壁

被记录的风暴
散发着油墨的气息
在记忆与遗忘的滚筒之间
报纸带着霉菌,上路

出 口

几乎所有的人
向我的梦中投掷石块
我和井水一起上升
那饥渴令人感动

他象警报一样惊醒
向着我们微笑
月亮牵着天空跳伞
在曙光的紧急出口处
他的签证已过期

BRIDGE

I'm adjusting the tape recorder's volume
——gradient of existence
sunlight and the ancient ideals
infuse various details, glimmer there

morning's boatman drifts through the wall

the storm being recorded
reeks of printer's ink
between the rollers of remembrance and forgetfulness
newspapers pick up mold, hit the streets

EXIT

for Donald Finkel

nearly everyone's
tossing stones into my dream
wellwater and I rise together
and people find that thirst moving

like an alarm startled awake
he's smiling at us
a moon leading the heavens away bails out of
dawn's emergency exit
where his visa's expired

Note: There's a saying in Chinese that if you fall
into a well, people will throw in stones.

战争状态

太阳密集地轰炸着大海
鲨鱼们在围攻下沉的岁月
那海底的银盘召唤家乡的传统:
带血的牛排,剥皮的土豆

进化史上不明的部分
是恋人们永远戒备的舌头
当密码严守人类的绝望
陌生的星球诞生了

荒草雇佣军占领了山谷
花朵缓慢地爆炸,树木生烟
我匍伏在诗歌后面
射击欢乐的鸟群

A STATE OF WAR

sunlight's hitting the sea with saturation bombing
sharks laying siege to the sinking years
that silver sea-floor platter calls to hometown traditions:
steak rare, potatoes peeled

what remains unclear in evolutionary history
is the lover's ever vigilant tongue
in that secret code guarding human hopelessness
a strange planet was born

mercenary weeds captured mountain valleys
blossoms casually detonate, trees smoke
I lie behind song
firing into cheery flocks of birds

无　题

苍鹰的影子掠过
麦田战栗

我成为夏天的解释者
回到大路上
戴上帽子集中思想

如果天空不死

UNTITLED

hawk shadow flickers past
fields of wheat shiver

I'm becoming one who explicates summer
return to the main road
put on a cap to concentrate thoughts

if deep skies never die

东方旅行者

早饭包括面包果酱奶油
和茶。我看窗外肥胖的鸽子
周围的客人动作迟缓
水族馆

我沿着气泡攀登

四匹花斑小马的精彩表演
它们期待的是燕麦
细细咀嚼时间的快乐

我沿着雷鸣的掌声攀登

推土机过后的夏天
我和一个陌生人交换眼色
死神是偷拍的大师
他借助某只眼睛
选取某个角度

我沿着陌生人的志向攀登

那自行车赛手表情变形
他无法停下来,退出急流
象弹钢琴的某个手指

我沿着旋律攀登

EASTERN TRAVELER

breakfast of toast butter jam
and tea. I watch a fat pigeon outside the window
guests all around in slow motion
an aquarium

I ascend the bubbles

four piebald ponies in a splendid performance
look forward to oats
and the pleasure of munching on time

I ascend the thunderous applause

in the summer after bulldozers
I exchange glances with a stranger
death's the great master of stolen shots
such a singular eye
choosing camera angles

I ascend the stranger's aspiration

that grimacing bicycle racer
can't stop, can't escape the fierce current
like a finger playing piano

I ascend the melody

某人在等火车时入睡
他开始了终点以后的旅行
电话录音机回答:
请在信号声响后留话

忧 郁

我乘电梯从地下停车场
升到海平线的位置
冥想继续上升,越过蓝色

象医生一样不可阻挡
他们,在决定我的一生:
通向成功的道路

男孩子的叫喊与季节无关
他在成长,他知道
怎样在梦里伤害别人

asleep while waiting for a train
someone sets out beyond his destination
the answering machine replies:
please leave a message after the beep

FORLORN

I take the elevator from an underground parking lot
up to sea level
deep thoughts continuing up, through blue color

like doctors you can't stop
them, deciding my whole life:
the road to success

the season's unrelated to a boy's shout
he's growing up, he knows
how to wound others in his dreams

夜巡

他们的天空,我的睡眠
黑暗中的演讲者

在冬天转车
在冬天转车
养蜂人远离他的花朵

另一个季节在停电
小小的祭品呵
不同声部的烛火

老去已不可能,老去的
半路,老虎回头——

NIGHT PATROL

their skies, my sleep
and orators in the midst of darkness

changing trains in winter
changing trains in winter
the beekeeper far from his flowers

in the power outage another season
o tiny offerings
candle flames in different parts of the chorus

grown old impossible, on that grown-old
road, a tiger turns back——

毒药

烟草屏住呼吸

流亡者的窗户对准
大海深处放飞的翅膀
冬日的音乐驶来
象褪色的旗帜

是昨天的风,是爱情

悔恨如大雪般降落
当一块石头裸露出结局
我以此刻痛哭余生

再给我一个名字

我伪装成不幸
遮挡母语的太阳

TOXIN

tobacco's breath catches short

an exile's window aims at
deep-sea wings released into flight
music of a winter's day sailing closer
like a flag shedding its colors

it's yesterday's wind, it's love

remorse deep as the fall of heavy snow
when a stone reveals the end result
I take this moment to weep for the rest of my life

give me another name

I've made a disguise of misfortune
shelter from the mother tongue's solar blaze

记 录

一只桔子偷运着死亡
人们三五成群
议论沉睡在他乡的黄金
和女人,警察敲门
道路在明天转身
重新核对着大事年表
而错误不可避免:
诗已诞生

RECORDS

when a tangerine's trafficking in death
men gather in threes and fours
talk of gold asleep in distant lands
and women, police knock on the door
tomorrow the road turns
rechecking the chronology of history
but mistakes can't be avoided
the poem is already born

在天涯

群山之间的爱情

永恒,正如万物的耐心
简化人的声音
一声凄厉的叫喊
从远古至今

休息吧,疲惫的旅行者
受伤的耳朵
暴露了你的尊严

一声凄厉的叫喊

AT THE SKY'S EDGE

love among the mountains

eternity, that patience of the earth
simplifies our human sounds
one arctic-thin cry
from deep antiquity until now

rest, weary traveler
a wounded ear's
already laid your dignity bare

one arctic-thin cry

除了明天

日子四处调查事故
我心静如水

那深入明天的河流
离开我,曝光

我爬上大雾的顶端了望
月光疑心重重

而道路必然存在
马蹄铁如不朽的诗章

OTHER THAN TOMORROW

day goes everywhere investigating accidents
but my head's quiet as water

that river flowing deep into tomorrow
sets out from me, exposure to light

I climb atop heavy fog and gaze out
suspicions of moonlight layered

but the road no doubt exists
and horseshoes like poems lasting forever

醒 悟

成群的乌鸦再次出现
冲向行军的树林

我在冬天的斜坡上醒来
梦在向下滑行

有时阳光仍保持
两只狗见面时的激动

那交响乐是一所医院
整理着尘世的混乱

老人突然撒手
一生织好的布匹

水涌上枝头
金属的玫瑰永不凋零

AWAKENING

flocks of crows appear once again
invading the marching forest

I come to on the slope of winter
dream gliding downhill

there are times sunlight still holds
the exhilaration of two dogs meeting

that symphony a hospital
sorting through this world of confusion

an old man suddenly lets go of that
cloth he spent a lifetime weaving

water wells up to the tips of branches
a metal rose never withers

播种者

一个播种者走进大厅
外面是战争，他说
而你沉湎于空虚
放弃警示危险的责任
我以田野的名义
外面是战争

我走出大厅
四周一片丰收的景象
我开始设计战争
表演死亡
被我点燃的庄稼
狼烟般升起

一个念头让我发疯:
他正在大理石上播种

SOWER

a sower walks into the great hall
it's war out there, he says
and you awash in emptiness
you've sworn off your duty to sound the alarm
I've come in the name of fields
it's war out there

I walk out from that great hall
all four directions a boundless harvest scene
I start planning for war
performing death
and the crops I burn
send up the wolf-smoke of warning fires

but something haunts me furiously:
he's sowing seed across marble floors

告别之词

转身向幸福
哦,陌生的立场
迁徙的时刻
谁能记住火焰的姿态
象变质的痛苦
笑,先于怜悯之情

清晨授权让我
公开此刻
谁能关上深渊之门
睡眠的定时器
让生者入睡
唤醒死者

FAREWELL WORDS

turning to face happiness
o, strange stance
migratory moment
who can remember flame's demeanor
like pain going bad
smiling, before pity begins

dawn's authority lets me
open this moment to the public
who is it can close that door to the abyss
that sleep-timer
lets the living enter sleep
and rouses the dead

风 景

乌云覆盖着功名
灯光在冷漠之夜上
刻花,从石头里
日子诞生
堆积成住所

你潜藏于喜悦
逼问秋天
使果实落满草地
我无法拒绝你
象一个谎言

蛀虫是个微雕大师
改变内部的风景

LANDSCAPE

dark clouds covering honor
lamplight cuts into the night of indifference
blossoms, and from the stone
days are born
piling up into a shelter

you hiding in happiness
interrogating autumn
and littering meadows with fruit
I cannot refuse you
like a lie

feeding moths are the masters of minute carving
transfiguring inner landscapes

新世纪

倾心于荣耀,大地转暗
我们读混凝土之书的
灯光,读真理

金子的炸弹爆炸
我们情愿成为受害者
把伤口展示给别人

考古学家会发现
底片上的时代幽灵
一个孩子抓住它,说不

是历史妨碍我们飞行
是鸟妨碍我们走路
是腿妨碍我们做梦

是我们诞生了我们
是诞生

A NEW CENTURY

in love with glory, the earth grows dark
reading the lights of a concrete
book, we read truth

solid gold bombs detonate
and we're glad to be victims
showing our wounds to the others

when archaeologists discover
the ghost of the era on a negative
a child grabs it, saying no

it's history that won't let us fly
it's birds that won't let us walk
it's legs that won't let us dream

it's our giving birth to ourselves
it's birth

问 天

今夜雨零乱
清风翻书
字典旁敲侧击
逼我就范

从小背古诗
不得要领
阐释的深渊旁
我被罚站

月朗星稀
老师的手从中
指点迷津
影子戏仿人生

有人在教育
的斜坡上滑雪
他们的故事
滑出国界

词滑出了书
白纸是遗忘症
我洗净双手
撕碎它,雨停

ASKING THE SKY

tonight a confusion of rain
fresh breezes leaf through the book
dictionaries swell with implication
forcing me into submission

memorizing ancient poems as a child
I couldn't see what they meant
and stood at the abyss of explication
for punishment

bright moon sparse stars
out of those depths a teacher's hands
give directions to the lost
a shadow mocking our lives

people slide down the slope of
education on skis
their story
slides beyond national boundaries

after words slide beyond the book
the white page is pure amnesia
I wash my hands clean
and tear it apart, the rain stops

夜匆匆

我们如易碎的器皿
必须注明：
朝上、小心

但我们并不怕水
象带伞的女人
外出,抵抗坏天气

给母亲的信
必经一生的路程
绕过敌意

有人在远方敲钟
唯一的钟
和明天争论

亡灵忙于接通电话
传递无主之词
我们在听

HEADLONG NIGHT

we're like fragile glassware
and need clear labeling:
this side up, handle with care

but we're not afraid of water
no more than a woman with her umbrella
heading outside, resisting bad weather

letters sent to mothers
must pass clear through life's journey
slipping around hostility

someone in a distant place rings a bell
solitary bell
arguing against tomorrow

a dead soul busily making phone calls
transmits ownerless words
and we listen

忠诚

别开灯
黑暗之门引来圣者

我的手熟知途径
象一把旧钥匙
在心的位置
打开你的命运

三月在门外飘动

几根竹子摇晃
有人正从地下潜泳
暴风雪已过
蝴蝶重新集结

我信仰般追随你
你追随死亡

ALLEGIANCE

don't turn the lights on
darkness is a door bringing the saint near

my hand knows the way perfectly
like an old key
at the heart-site
opening your destiny

March flutters outside the door

a few bamboo sway
people snorkeling underground
now the snowstorm's passed
butterflies gather again

it's my faith to be following you
you following death

无 题

在母语的防线上
奇异的乡愁
垂死的玫瑰

玫瑰用茎管饮水
如果不是水
至少是黎明

最终露出午夜
疯狂的歌声
披头散发

UNTITLED

at the mother tongue's line of defense
a strange homesickness
a dying rose

rose sipping water via stem-tubing
or if it isn't water
it's at least dawn light

revealing midnight in the end
wild song
flurried head of hair

如歌的行板

1

小号是乐队指挥的心腹
连接灯光,刺探夜色
并证明:神不在场

2

云中的火枪手保持沉默
政治家的诺言和失眠和短裤
露出古老的车站
铁轨一直抵达民族的老年
仇恨的的程度不变

3

凝视的灯光抽搐

4

在旅馆中醒来
我成为本世纪多余的一夜
痛饮,酒使我透明

时间在书中崩溃了

刀光剑影
逼风暴显形
溢美之词
逼一位上司引咎辞职
在通往表达之路上

ANDANTE

1

the trumpet is a conductor's conspirator
assembling light, scouting dark night
and testifying: no gods in sight

2

musketeers keep silence in clouds
bermuda shorts and insomnias and promises of statesmen
reveal that age-old station
rails running straight through to a nation's old age
the degree of hate never changes

3

a fixed gaze of light is twitching

4

coming to in the hotel
I become a spare night the century doesn't need
and drink up again, wine rendering me transparent

time's crumbled inside the book

knives glinting and swords flashing
compel the storm to reveal itself
flattering words
compel the boss to take responsibility and abdicate
on the road toward self-expression

5

蝉声如对手

在无人的集市上
灾祸和我一起叫喊
念头邪恶的蘑菇
破土而出

6

一对盲情人拐过街角
城市的舞台转动

5

cicada song's a rival

in deserted markets
catastrophe and I cry out together
mushrooms of demonic thought
breaking ground emerge

6

blind lovers turn a sheet corner
the urban stage revolves

折叠方法

猫回到原处

战争之鱼
跃过牧师的天空
女高音隐退

我回到原处

虚妄之沙
扑向玻璃窗
那乌云的面具

石头回到原处

幸运之梦
长成参天巨树
象墨汁渗入地图

意义回到原处

欺世之虹
是伟人的自传
他一步跨向童年

FOLDING PROCEDURE

cats return to where they began

battle fish
leap beyond clerical heavens
and the soprano goes into seclusion

I return to where I began

quixotic sand
hurls itself against window-glass
that mask of dark cloud

stones return to where they began

dreams of good fortune
grow into trees towering skyward
like ink seeping into the map

meanings return to where they began

the rainbow deluding this world
is a glorious person's autobiography
he steps back into childhood

遭遇

他们煮熟了种子
绕过历史,避开战乱
深入夜的矿层
成为人民

在洞穴的岩画上
我触摸到他们
挖掘的手指
欲望的耻骨
回溯源头的努力

仅在最后一步
他们留在石壁中
拒我在外

我走出洞穴
汇入前进的人流

ENCOUNTER

they cooked the seed
bypassed history, eluded turmoil and war
plunged deep into the mineral seam of night
and became a people

in paintings on cave walls
I come upon them
their digging fingers
pubic-bones of longing
that struggle to retrace origins

right up to the last step
where they remain in rock walls
leaving me to the outside

I walk from the cave
mingling into the people advancing

闪光

清凉之水漫过青苔
鸟啼不绝,如投石在水中
阵雨在测量天地
石头呼唤石头
诡秘的时刻互相摩擦
闪电是再生之路
花朵冷热自知,闭合
谛听内心的声音

FLASH

pure-cold water brims over green moss
bird calls open endlessly, stones thrown into water
scattered showers are mapping heaven and earth
stone calls out to stone
and clandestine moments wear against each other
a flash of lightning is the road to a new life
buds know themselves through hot and cold, closed
listening closely to the heart-sound

夏季指南

如隐身的匠人敲打金箔
大海骤然生辉——
船只四出追逐夜色
带着灯,那天使们的水晶

鸥群进行着神秘的运算
结果永远是那受伤的一只
风吹起它奄拉的羽毛
夸大了这一垂死的事实

峭崖象手风琴般展开
回声,使做爱的人们发狂
岸上唯一的古堡
和海中的映象保持对称

A GUIDE TO SUMMER

as if beaten into gold foil by invisible artisans
the sea suddenly breaks into light——
fleets chasing night set out in all directions
carrying lights, those crystals of angels

flocks of gulls perform mystical calculations
and the result is forever one casualty
wind raising its limp feathers
making more of this one dying fact

sheer accordion-spread canyons
echo, driving naked lovers into hysterics
an old castle on the coast
maintains symmetry with its image at sea

变奏

云在行进,公共汽车里
一个男人在报纸后面微笑
象读圣经的上帝

司机的心脏发出轰鸣
上坡,又滑向隧道

灯光是切分音
我进入集体的睡眠
穿过狗的骨头和关节

登堂入室,我升华

MUSICAL VARIATIONS

clouds are advancing, on the bus
a man smiles behind his newspaper
like a god reading his bible

the driver's heart roars
uphill, and slips on toward the tunnel

amid syncopated streetlights
I enter communal sleep
drifting through dog-bones and dog-joints

into higher rooms of achievement, I rise in sublimation

一幅肖像

为信念所伤,他来自八月
那危险的母爱
被一面镜子夺去
他侧身于犀牛与政治之间
象裂缝隔开时代

哦同谋者,我此刻
只是一个普通的游客
在博物馆大厅的棋盘上
和别人交叉走动

激情不会过时
但访问必须秘密进行
我突然感到那琴弦的疼痛
你调音,为我奏一曲
在众兽涌入历史之前

A PORTRAIT

wounded by convictions, he came from August
a mother's perilous love
stolen away by a mirror
he's sideways between the rhinoceros and politics
like a fissure separating epochs

o conspirators, I'm nothing now
but a common wanderer
walking the cavernous museum's chessboard
trading places with strangers

great passion's never outdated
but our visits require secrecy
suddenly I feel the ache of strings
you're tuning, play me a song
before predators emerge into history

田园诗

音乐之狼迂回奔跑
山楂们吃吃窃笑

翻过一页,退潮
阳台上年幼的船长们
用望远镜眺望

东方与西方
一个切成两半的水果

我挂网捕鸟
在自己吐核栽种的
树下,等了多年

PASTORAL

wolves of music weave their way at a run
hawthorns wheeze with clandestine laughter

turning a new leaf, tide's out
young ship-captains on a balcony
look far away through telescopes

east and west
a single fruit cut into halves

beneath a tree grown from the pit I spit out
I've hung nets to
trap birds, and waited many years

关于永恒

从众星租来的光芒下
长跑者穿过死城

和羊谈心
我们共同分享美酒
和桌下的罪行

雾被引入夜歌
炉火如伟大的谣言
迎向风

如果死是爱的理由
我们爱不贞之情
爱失败的人
那察看时间的眼睛

ON ETERNITY

beneath a radiance rented from the stars
long-distance runners transit death's city

chatting heart-to-heart with sheep
we share a lovely wine
and under-the-table crime

fog's lured into night-song
and stove-fire like mighty rumor
greets the wind

if death's the reason for love
we love unfaithful passion
love the defeated
those eyes gazing into time

Bei Dao is by now well-known as the most prominent literary voice in China's political opposition. His work has been not a matter of overt political statement, but the rescue of subjectivity from a government that depends on its suppression. To do this, Bei Dao has employed increasingly surreal procedures, procedures he speaks of as opening a space in official discourse, in the program dictating how people live and think and feel.

However derived from Western poetics his work may at first seem, Bei Dao's very different cultural context allowed him to use surrealist techniques for his own unique purposes. The more private and introspective his work became, the more subversively political it was. Indeed, the use of such a strange, foreign language made Bei Dao's voice seem to come out of nowhere, and this alone was so threatening that the government felt compelled to suppress it. Individuality is the mysterious space where political freedom and self-determination become conceivable. But it was perhaps this space itself, more than the political revolution it makes possible, that the protesters were demanding at Tiananmen Square.

In 1989, when the opposition was crushed at Tiananmen, Bei Dao found himself exiled in the West. Wandering from country to country, he has taken on an increasingly international role as spokesman for the individual and the disenfranchised. As before, rather than addressing the social and political situation in a direct way, he recreates the fragmented experience that situation allows us, experience for which conventional language seems inadequate. Bei Dao's work recalls China's ancient masters: clear resonant images set in sharp juxtapositions. But his are decidedly modern clarities, adrift on the terrible mystery of today's world-historical forces. His poems are constructed from splinters of a civilization frittering itself away in a ruins of the spirit; and at the same time, in the private space they create, the poems open forms of distance from those ruins.

David Hinton
East Calais, Vermont
January 1994

Landscape Over Zero

Translated by David Hinton
with Yanbing Chen

抵达

那时我们还年轻
疲倦得象一只瓶子
等待愤怒升起

哦岁月的愤怒

火光羞惭啊黑夜永存
在书中出生入死
圣者展现了冬天的意义

哦出发的意义

汇合着的啜泣抬头
大声叫喊
被主所遗忘

ARRIVAL

we were still young then
tired as some bottle
waiting for anger to rise

o anger of the years

firelight shamed o dark night alive forever
migrating in books through life and death
sages reveal the meaning of winter

o meaning of going forth

gathering sobs look up
scream out
in their god's amnesia

另一个

这棋艺平凡的天空
看海水变色
楼梯深入镜子
盲人学校里的手指
触摸鸟的消亡

这闲置冬天的桌子
看灯火明灭
记忆几度回首
自由射手们在他乡
听历史的风声

某些人早已经匿名
或被我们阻拦在
地平线以下
而另一个在我们之间
突然嚎啕大哭

ANOTHER

this sky unexceptional at chess
watches the sea change color
a ladder goes deep into the mirror
fingers in a school for the blind
touch the extinction of birds

look at those flickering lights
on winter's fallow table
memory looks back a few times
the archer of freedom in foreign lands
listen to history's wind

some abandoned their names long ago
or we stalled them
under the horizon
meanwhile another among us
bursts into tears

蓝 墙

道路追问天空

一只轮子
寻找另一只轮子作证：

这温暖的皮毛
闪电之诗
生殖和激情
此刻或缩小的全景
无梦

是汽油的欢乐

BLUE WALL

road chases sky asking

one wheel
seeks another to bear witness

this pelt of warmth
poetry of lightning
procreation and passion
this very moment or whole vistas reduced
dreamless

are gasoline's thrills

创 造

世世代代的创造令我不安
例如夜在法律上奔走
总有一种原因
一只狗向着雾狂吠
船在短波中航行
被我忘记了的灯塔
如同拔掉的牙不再疼痛
翻飞的书搅乱了风景
太阳因得救而升起
那些人孤独得踩着脚排队
一阵钟声为他们押韵

除此以外还剩下什么
霞光在玻璃上大笑
电梯下降，却没有地狱
一个被国家辞退的人
穿过昏热的午睡
来到海滩，潜入水底

CREATION

all those generations being created rob me of peace
night for instance scurries around above the law
never without reason
a dog barks wildly at fog
ships sail on shortwave
the lighthouse I've forgotten
painless as a pulled tooth
fluttering books spoil the scenery
the sun rises by being salvaged
people there so lonely they stand in line stamping their feet
a bell tolling for them providing the rhyme

what is it remains beyond this
twilight laughs out loud on glass
the elevator descends, but there's no hell
someone the country's discharged
passes through a stifling-hot midday nap
reaches a beach, dives down deep

完整

在完整的一天的尽头
一些搜寻爱情的小人物
在黄昏留下了伤痕

必有完整的睡眠
天使在其中关怀某些
开花的特权

当完整的罪行进行时
钟表才会准时
火车才会开动

琥珀里完整的火焰
战争的客人们
围着它取暖

冷场,完整的月亮升起
一个药剂师在配制
剧毒的时间

PERFECT

at the end of a perfect day
those simple people looking for love
left scars on twilight

there must be a perfect sleep
in which angels tend certain
blossoming privileges

when the perfect crime happens
clocks will be on time
trains will start moving

a perfect flame in amber
war's guests
gather around it keeping warm

stage hushed, perfect moon rising
the pharmacist is preparing
a total poison of time

背 景

必须修改背景
你才能够重返故乡

时间撼动了某些字
起飞，又落下
没透露任何消息
一连串的失败是捷径
穿过大雪中寂静的看台
逼向老年的大钟

而一个家庭宴会的高潮
和酒精的含量有关
离你最近的女人
总是带着历史的愁容
注视着积雪、空行

田鼠们所坚信的黑暗

BACKGROUND

the background needs revising
you can return to your hometown

a few time-shaken words
lift into flight, fall back
divulging no news whatsoever
a string of failures is the shortcut
past silent grandstands in heavy snow
pressing toward the huge clock of old age

at the family gathering
high tide is a matter of alcohol content
the woman closest to you
always wears the worried look of history
gazes into snowdrifts, double space to

darkness in which voles believe absolutely

无 题

在父亲平坦的想象中
孩子们固执的叫喊
终于撞上了高山
不要惊慌
我沿着某些树的想法
从口吃转向歌唱

来自远方的悲伤
是一种权力
我用它锯桌子
有人为了爱情出发
而一座宫殿追随风暴
驶过很多王朝

带家具的生活
以外, 跳蚤擂动大鼓
道士们练习升天
青春深入小巷
为夜的逻辑而哭
我得到休息

UNTITLED

in the plains of a father's imagination
insistent cries of children
strike high peaks in the end
don't panic
tracing thoughts of certain trees
I stutter into song

sorrow from far away
is a kind of power
I use it to saw tables
someone sets out for the sake of love
and a palace following storms
sails through many dynasties

beyond life with home
furnishings, fleas beat a huge drum
Taoists practice their ascent into heaven
youth goes deep into back alleys
weeping over the logic of night
I attain rest

这一天

风熟知爱情
夏日闪烁着皇家的颜色
钓鱼人孤独地测量
大地的伤口
敲响的钟在膨胀
午后的漫步者
请加入这岁月的含义

有人俯向钢琴
有人扛着梯子走过
睡意被推迟了几分钟
仅仅几分钟
太阳在研究阴影
我从明镜饮水
看见心目中的敌人

男高音的歌声
象油轮激怒大海
我凌晨三时打开罐头
让那些鱼大放光明

THIS DAY

wind knows what love is
the summer day flashing royal colors
a lone fisherman surveys
the world's wound
a struck bell swells
people strolling in the afternoon
please join the year's implications

someone bends toward a piano
someone carries a ladder past
sleepiness has been postponed a few minutes
only a few minutes
the sun researches shadow
and drinking water from a bright mirror
I see the enemy within

an oil tanker
the tenor's song enrages the sea
at three in the morning I open a tin can
setting some fish on fire

二月

夜正趋于完美
我在语言中漂流
死亡的乐器
充满了冰

谁在日子的裂缝上
歌唱，水变苦
火焰失血
山猫般奔向星星
必有一种形式
才能做梦

在早晨的寒冷中
一只觉醒的鸟
更接近真理
而我和我的诗
一起下沉

书中的二月：
某些动作与阴影

FEBRUARY

night approaching perfection
I float amid languages
the brasses in death's music
full of ice

who's up over the crack in day
singing, water turns bitter
bled flames pale
leaping like leopards toward stars
to dream
you need a form

in the cold morning
an awakened bird
comes closer to truth
as I and my poems
sink together

february in the book:
certain movements and shadows

进 程

日复一日，苦难
正如伟大的事业般衰败
象一个小官僚
我坐在我的命运中
点亮孤独的国家

死者没有朋友
盲目的煤，嘹亮的灯光
我走在我的疼痛上
围栏以外的羊群
似田野开绽

形式的大雨使石头
变得残破不堪
我建造我的年代
孩子们凭借一道口令
穿过书的防线

PROGRESS

day after day, misery
fails like some great venture
I sit within my fate
like a small-time bureaucrat
lighting a lonely country

the dead have no friends
blind coal, resonant lamplight
I walk above my pain
herds of sheep outside the fence
as if fields were breaking open

the heavy rains of form change stone
into utter ruins
I construct my time
children using a password
penetrate the book's defenses

我们

失魂落魄
提着灯笼追赶春天

伤疤发亮，杯子转动
光线被创造
看那迷人的时刻：
盗贼潜入邮局
信发出叫喊

钉子啊钉子
这歌词不可更改
木柴紧紧搂在一起
寻找听众

寻找冬天的心
河流尽头
船夫等待着茫茫暮色

必有人重写爱情

we

lost souls and scattered spirits
holding lanterns chase spring

scars shimmer, cups revolve
light's being created
look at that enchanting moment
a thief steals into a post office
letters cry out

nails o nails
the lyrics never change
firewood huddles together
searching for an audience to listen

searching for the heart of winter
river's end
a boatman awaiting boundless twilight

there must be someone to rewrite love

出 场

语病盛开的童年
我们不多说
闲逛人生
看栅栏后的大海
我们搭乘过的季节
跃入其中

音乐冷酷无比
而婚姻错落有致
一个厌世者
走向确切的地址
如烟消散

无尽的悲哀之浪
催孩子们起床
阳光聚散
我们不多说

SHOWING UP

in childhoods of broken grammar blooming
we don't say much
roam life
watch oceans beyond fences
seasons by which we traveled
plunge in

music perfectly cold and cruel
marriage neatly strewn
someone sick of this world
walks toward a definite address
like smoke vanishing

endless waves of sorrow
hurry children out of bed
sunlight gathers & scatters
we don't say much

在歧路

从前的日子痛斥
此刻的花朵
那使青春骄傲的夜
抱着石头滚动
击碎梦中的玻璃

我为何在此逗留?
中年的书信传播着
浩大的哀怨
从不惑之鞋倒出
沙子，或计谋

没有任何准备
在某次会议的陈述中
我走得更远
沿着一个虚词拐弯
和鬼魂们一起
在歧路迎接日落

ON THE WRONG ROAD

days gone-by rail against
the moment's flower
night that does youth proud
tumbles hugging stones
breaking glass in dreams

why linger on here?
mid-life letters circulate
vast sorrows
shoes of certainty pour out
sand, or schemes

completely unprepared
I walk further out
in some statement at a conference
tracing the twist in a preposition
joining ghosts
on the wrong road to greet sunset

明 镜

夜半饮酒时
真理的火焰发疯
回首处
谁没有家
窗户为何高悬

你倦于死
道路倦于生
在那火红的年代
有人昼伏夜行
与民族对弈

并不止于此
挖掘你睡眠的人
变成蓝色
早晨倦于你
明镜倦于词语

想想爱情
你有如壮士
惊天动地之处
你对自己说
太冷

BRIGHT MIRROR

in the midnight hour of wine
the flame of truth gets crazy
a place for looking back
who has no home
why do windows loom so high

you're tired of death
the road's tired of life
in those flame-red times
someone rests by day and travels by night
playing chess with a nation

but that's not all
people excavating your sleep
turn blue
morning's tired of you
the bright mirror's tired of words

think about love
and you're like some hero
where heaven trembles and earth shakes
you say to yourself
too cold

早晨

那些鱼内脏如灯
又亮了一次

醒来，口中含盐
好似初尝喜悦

我出去散步
房子学会倾听

一些树转身
某人成了英雄

必须用手势问候
鸟和打鸟的人

MORNING

those fish entrails as if lights
blink again

waking, there's salt in my mouth
just like the first taste of joy

I go out for a walk
houses learning to listen

a few trees turn around
and someone's become a hero

you must use hand gestures to greet
birds and the hunters of birds

无 题

行人们点亮自己
脑袋里的灯泡
大街奔向十月的狂想

向一只狗致敬
影子斜向它的经验

泉水暴露了
风景以下的睡眠
我们轮流伏在
长明的窗下哭泣

李白击鼓而歌
从容不迫

UNTITLED

pedestrians lighting their own
light-bulb minds
the street heads for october's wild ideas

in tribute to a dog
shadow leans toward its experience

spring water's laid bare
the sleep underlying landscapes
we take turns hiding beneath
windows of endless light weeping

Li Po beats a drum and sings
calm and unhurried

新手

新手的夜晚
无所畏惧
他们在房顶齐声朗读
一纸无字的黄昏
他们在大雪的债务
和马的喘息中
接近开花的地点
他们在时代广场上
著书立说
用长鞭触及意义
在水泥裂缝
种自己的名字

日子被折叠起来
还剩下什么
随生死起伏的歌声
必将返回到他们
张大而无声的嘴巴中

NOVICE

novice evenings
nothing to fear
they recite on rooftops in one voice
that page of wordless twilight
out on snowstorm debts
and the gasping of tired horses
they approach a site that's blooming
and out on that time square
they produce books and schools of thought
use long whips to touch meanings
sow their names
along cracks in the concrete

days get folded up
what remains
the song tracing life's rise and fall
returns inevitably to their
gaping mouths of silence

重 影

谁在月下敲门
看石头开花
琴师在回廊游荡
令人砰然心动
不知朝夕
流水和金鱼
拨动时光方向

向日葵受伤
指点路径
盲人们站在
不可理解之光上
抓住愤怒
刺客与月亮
一起走向他乡

SEEING DOUBLE

who knocks on a door in moonlight
watching stone bloom
a musician wanders the corridors
it makes your heart pound
not knowing if it's morning or night
flowing water and goldfish
adjust the direction of time

a wounded sunflower
points the way
the blind stand on
light beyond understanding
clutching anger
assassin and moon
walk toward a foreign land

领 域

今夜始于何处
客人们在墙上干杯
妙语与灯周旋

谁苦心练习
演奏自己的一生
那秃头钢琴家
家里准有一轮太阳

模仿沉默
我的手爬过桌子

有人把狗赶进历史
再挖掘出来
它们把住大门
一对老人转身飞走
回头时目光凶狠

二月召来乡下木匠
重新支撑天空
道路以外的春天
让人忙于眺望

REALM

where did tonight begin
guests toast on the wall
their wit sparring the light

practicing relentlessly
to perform his own life
the bald pianist
clearly keeps a full sun at home

imitating silence
my hand crawls across the desk

people chase dogs into history
then excavate
and make them gatekeepers
an old couple turns and hurries away
looking back with a savage gaze

february summons country carpenters
to prop up the sky anew
and springtime beyond the road
keeps us busy with the long view

据我所知

前往那故事中的人们
搬开了一座大山
他才诞生

我从事故出发
刚抵达另一个国家
颠倒字母
使每餐必有意义

掂脚够着时间的刻度
战争对他还太远
父亲又太近
他低头通过考试
踏上那无边的甲板

隔墙有耳
但我要跟上他的速度
写作!

他用红色油漆道路
让凤凰们降落
展示垂死的动作
那些含义不明的路标
环绕着冬天
连音乐都在下雪

AS FAR AS I KNOW

people on the way to that story
moved a mountain
then he was born

setting out from the accident
I barely reached another country
turning alphabets upside down
to fill every meal with meaning

he reaches up to the scale measuring time
war remains too far away
father too close
he stoops to pass through exams
and boards that boundless boatdeck

someone's listening behind walls
I must hurry to keep up with him
writing!

he paints the road red
lets phoenixes land
flaunting death throes
those incoherent roadsigns
surround winter
snow falling even from music

我小心翼翼
每个字下都是深渊

当一棵大树
平息着八面来风
他的花园
因妄想而荒芜

我漫不经心地翻看
他的不良记录
只能坚信过去的花朵

他伪造了我的签名
而长大成人
并和我互换大衣
以潜入我的夜
搜寻着引爆故事的
导火索

I'm careful very careful
there's an abyss beneath every word

when a huge tree
quiets wind from the eight directions
his flower garden
is desolated by fantasy

I leaf carelessly through
his bad record
nothing to believe but the past's flower

he forged my signature
and grew into a man
traded coats with me
and stole into my night
searching out the story's detonation
fuse

主题

早晨的碗
一生中的朋友
让我回味那种恩惠
而我被门所否认

关于生活会另有解释
很多书在鼓掌
并追随阴郁的革命
埋藏着狐狸骨头

我向西再向东
回避着主题
夜的滑翔机展开
序曲中交错的目光

风景依旧
那群逃税的大象狂奔
政策背道而驰
农民们洗耳恭听

岁月起伏的地方
我摸索着回家
楼上有人打开窗户
泼出了一盆脏水

THEME

a morning bowl
lifelong friend
lets me savor such kindness
and yet doors deny me

there will be other ways of explaining life
many books are applauding
they follow the dismal revolution
burying fox bones

I head west and then east
avoiding the theme
the sailplane of night opening out
crisscross glances in the overture

same scenery as ever
that herd of tax-evading elephants runs wild
official policy hurries in the opposite direction
peasants clean their ears and listen politely

where years rise and fall
I grope my way home
someone upstairs opens a window
and empties a pan of dirty water

守 夜

月光小于睡眠
河水穿过我们的房间
家具在哪儿靠岸

不仅是编年史
也包括非法的气候中
公认的一面
使我们接近雨林
哦哭泣的防线

玻璃镇纸读出
文字叙述中的伤口
多少黑山挡住了
一九四九年

在无名小调的尽头
花握紧拳头叫喊

NIGHTWATCH

moonlight smaller than sleep
the river flows through our room
where is furniture docking

not only annals of history
but also the illicit climate's
acknowledged aspects
bring us to rain forests
o line of defense in tears

glass paperweights decode
writing's wound of narration
how many black mountains blocked
1949

where a nameless tune ends
blossoms scream clenched fists

无 题

——给Martin Mooij

集邮者们窥视生活
欢乐一闪而过

夜傲慢地跪下
托起世代的灯火

风转向，鸟发狂
歌声摇落多少苹果

不倦的情人白了头
我俯身看命运

泉水安慰我
在这无用的时刻

UNTITLED

—for Martin Mooij

stamp collectors peer at life
happiness a flash suddenly gone

arrogant night kneels down
holding up the lights of generations

winds shifts direction, birds crazed
song shaking down how many apples

the hair of tireless lovers turned white
I bend down to look at fate

springwater comforts me
in such useless moments

无 题

人们赶路，到达
转世，隐入鸟之梦
太阳从麦田逃走
又随乞丐返回

谁与天比高
那早夭的歌手
在气象图里飞翔
掌灯冲进风雪

我买了份报纸
从日子找回零钱
在夜的入口处
摇身一变

被颂扬之鱼
穿过众人的泪水
喂，上游的健康人
到明天有多远

UNTITLED

people hurry on, arrive
return in another life, fade into bird dreams
the sun flees wheat fields
then comes back trailing after beggars

who's rivaled sky for height
that singer who died young
soars in the weather map
flies into snowstorms holding a lamp

I bought a newspaper
got change back from the day
and at the entrance to night
eased into a new identity

celebrated fish
move through everyone's tears
hey, you folks upstream achievers so hale and hearty
how far is it to tomorrow

夜

充满细节的排浪
我们以外之光
正是想象来自伤口
月亮护士穿行
为每颗心上发条

我们笑了
在水中摘下胡子
从三个方向记住风
自一只蝉的高度
看寡妇的世界

夜比所有的厄运
更雄辩
夜在我们脚下
这遮蔽诗的灯罩
已经破碎

NIGHT

surf crowded with detail
the light beyond us
it's imagination come of wounds
nurse moon meanders
winding each heart's mainspring

we laughed
pulled off beards in the water
remembered wind in three directions
and from the altitude of a cicada
watched the widow's world

night's more eloquent than
all bad fortune
night under our feet
this lampshade over the poem
already shattered

紫色

明亮的下午
号角阵阵
满树的柿子晃动
如知识在脑中
我开门等夜
在大师的时间里
读书，下棋
有人从王位上
扔出石头

没有击中我
船夫幽灵般划过
波光创造了你
并为你纹身
我们手指交叉
一颗星星刹住车
照亮我们

PURPLE

bright afternoon
the bugle call over and over
persimmons filling trees sway
like knowledge in the mind
I open the door to await night
and in a sage-master's time
read books, play chess
someone on a throne
throws a rock

doesn't hit me
spectral boatmen row past
ripple-light creates you
etches your skin
our fingers intertwine
a star puts on the brakes
shines all over us

山中一日

九月向西
虚无的鸽子向东
光和马的细腿
在抄着近路
尝遍种子而无梦
我在向阳坡
练习飞翔
仅仅为了沉睡

为了醒来
钟敲十二下
午夜落叶
白昼生烟

A DAY IN THE MOUNTAINS

september heads west
the dove of nothingness heads east
thin legs of light and horses
are taking a shortcut
having tasted every seed and without dreams
I use a sunlit slope
to practice soaring
if only for sleep

for waking
the clock strikes twelve
midnight drops its leaves
daylight smolders

无 题

几度诗中回首
夜鸟齐鸣
你向歌声逝去之处
释放着烟雾

打伞进入明天
你，漫游者
从你的尽头再向前
什么能替代喜悦

世纪的狐狸们
在鸿沟之间跳跃
你看见那座辉煌的桥
怎样消失在天边

一个早晨触及
核桃隐秘的思想
水的激情之上
是云初醒时的孤独

UNTITLED

looking back a few times in the poem
night birds singing together
you set smoke drifting free
toward a place where song vanishes

walking into tomorrow beneath an umbrella
you, a wanderer
set out from your own end
what can replace joy

the century's foxes
leap from abyss to abyss
you see how that glorious bridge
dissappears at the sky's edge

morning touches
the secret thought of a walnut
above the passion of water
it's the loneliness of cloud waking

旧 地

死亡总是从反面
观察一幅画

此刻我从窗口
看见我年轻时的落日
旧地重游
我急于说出真相
可在天黑前
又能说出什么

饮过词语之杯
更让人干渴
与河水一起援引大地
我在空山倾听
吹笛人内心的呜咽

税收的天使们
从画的反面归来
从那些镀金的头颅
一直清点到落日

OLD PLACES

death's always on the other side
watching the painting

at the window just now
I saw a sunset from my youth
visiting old places again
I'm anxious to tell the truth
but before the skies go dark
what more can be said

drinking a cup of words
only makes you thirstier
I join riverwater to quote the earth
and listen in empty mountains
to the flute player's sobbing heart

angels collecting taxes
return from the painting's other side
from those gilded skulls
taking inventory clear into sunset

局外人

一代人如帷幕落下
下一代人在鼓掌

置身于暗处的人
你经历的时间
正得到重视
摸索，于是有光
让一半生命空出来
充满鹤鸣

有人在病中游泳
当秋风察看
幼兽小小的脾气
道路加入睡眠
在打败你的光线中
你坚守无名栅栏

OUTSIDER

one generation drops like a curtain
the next is applauding

the lifetime you've known
hiding in dark places
starts gaining attention
groping, hence light
letting half a life empty out
and fill with crane song

someone's swimming in sickness
as autumn wind inspects
the small temperaments of young animals
the road joins sleep
and in radiant light that's defeated you
you stand fast at the nameless fence

下一棵树

风从哪儿来
我们数着罂粟籽中的
日日夜夜

大雪散布着
某一气流的谎言
邮筒醒来
信已改变含义
道路通向历史以外
我们牵回往事
拴在下一棵树上

来吧，野蛮人
请加入这一传说
这预订的时刻开花
谦卑的火焰
变成他乡之虎

我们游遍四方
总是从下一棵树出发
返回，为了命名
那路上的忧伤

THE NEXT TREE

where is it wind comes from
we count days and nights passing
inside poppy seeds

a huge snowstorm spreads
that lie a certain flow of air tells
a mailbox wakes
letters already meaning something else
the road leads somewhere beyond history
we shepherd old memories out
and hitch them to the next tree

come, you barbarians
please join this legend
this moment reserved in advance blooms
humble flames
becoming a tiger in a foreign land

we've traveled everywhere
always setting out from the next tree
and returning, just to name
that sorrow of the road

为了

不眠之灯引导着你
从隐蔽的棋艺中
找到对手

歌声兜售它的影子
你从某个结论
走向开放的黎明
为什么那最初的光线
让你如此不安？

一颗被种进伤口的
种子拒绝作证：
你因期待而告别
因爱而受苦

激情，正如轮子
因闲置而完美

FOR THE PURPOSE OF

a sleepless lamp leads you
to search out an opponent
in the hidden art of chess

song peddles its shadow
from a certain conclusion
you walk toward the opening dawn
why is it the earliest gleam
makes you so anxious?

a seed planted inside wounds
refuses to bear witness
you leave whenever you expect more
suffer whenever you love

passion, just like a wheel
grows perfect whenever it's idle

无 题

当语言发疯，我们
在法律的一块空地上
因聋哑而得救
一辆辆校车
从光的深渊旁驶过
夜是一部旧影片
琴声如雨浸润了时代

孤儿们追逐着蓝天
服丧的书肃立
在通往阐释之路上
杜鹃花及姐妹们
为死亡而开放

UNTITLED

when language was insane, we
stood in the law's one vacant lot
and being deaf and dumb were saved
one school bus after another
skirts past an abyss of light
night's an old movie
and music soaks into the age like rain

as orphans chase blue sky
books stand in mourning
on the road leading to explanation
azalea and her sisters
bloom for death

失 眠

你在你的窗外看你
一生的光线变幻

因嫉妒而瞎了眼
星星逆风而行
在死亡的隐喻之外
展开道德的风景

在称为源泉的地方
夜终于追上了你
那失眠的大军
向孤独的旗帜致敬

辗转的守夜人
点亮那朵惊恐之花
猫纵身跃入长夜
梦的尾巴一闪

INSOMNIA

you see yourself outside your window
a lifetime's gleam in flux

gone blind out of jealousy
stars sail against the wind
beyond death's metaphor
and unfold ethical landscapes

in what is called a place of wellsprings
night finally catches up to you
that army of insomnia
salutes the flag of solitude

a nightwatchman tossing and turning
lights up that terror-blossom
a cat leaps into endless night
the dream's tail flashing once

零度以上的风景

是鹞鹰教会歌声游泳
是歌声追溯那最初的风

我们交换欢乐的碎片
从不同的方向进入家庭

是父亲确认了黑暗
是黑暗通向经典的闪电

哭泣之门砰然关闭
回声在追赶它的叫喊

是笔在绝望中开花
是花反抗着必然的旅程

是爱的光线醒来
照亮零度以上的风景

LANDSCAPE OVER ZERO

it's hawk teaching song to swim
it's song tracing back to the first wind

we trade scraps of joy
enter family from different directions

it's a father confirming darkness
it's darkness leading to that lightning of the classics

a door of weeping slams shut
echoes chasing its cry

it's a pen blossoming in lost hope
it's a blossom resisting the inevitable route

it's love's gleam waking to
light up landscape over zero

故 事

少年的喇叭盲目的回声
饮水的城市吐露真情
专家们攀登着夜的高压电
警察只出现过一次
在毫无意义的笑声中

语法里的狗叫浪的叹息
电话亭在海边做梦
一条鱼一种理由召来风暴
管风琴冒着烟流星飞溅
颂扬的是死去的一年

我沿着主要情节线
到达作者开始构思的地方
泪水中看见酒后的太阳
油漆未干的四月
蜂群引导饥饿的意象

STORY

children's trumpet blind echo
a water-drinking city tells the truth
experts climb night's high voltage
police appeared only once
in meaningless laughter

grammar's inner bark tidal sighs
a phonebooth dreams beside the sea
a fish a reason summoning storms
a pipe-organ smokes meteors spatter
what's praised is a dead year

I follow the main plot
to where an author's conception began
see a drunken sun through tears
wet-paint April
bees leading out images of hunger

不对称

历史的诡计之花开放
忙于演说的手指受伤
攒下来的阳光成为年龄
你沉于往事和泡沫
埋葬愤怒的工具
一个来自过去的陌生人
从镜子里指责你

而我所看到的是
守城的昏鸦正一只只死去
教我呼吸和意义的老师
在我写作的阴影咳血
那奔赴节日的衣裙
随日蚀或完美的婚姻
升起，没有歌声

ASYMMETRY

the blossom of history's ruse opens
fingers busy with talk are wounded
hoarded sunlight becomes age
you drown in times past and bubbles
bury anger's tools
a stranger out of the past
chides you from the mirror

though what I've seen is
the city's dusky guardian-crows dying one by one
and those who taught me breath and meaning
coughing up blood in shadows my writing casts
dresses rushing toward holidays
follow solar eclipse and perfect marriage
& rise, songless

蜡

青春期的蜡
深藏在记忆的锁内
火焰放弃了酒
废墟上的匆匆过客
我们的心

我们的心
会比恨走得更远
夜拒绝明天的读者
被点燃的蜡烛
晕眩得象改变天空的
一阵阵钟声
此刻唯一的沉默

此刻唯一的沉默
是裸露的花园
我们徒劳地卷入其中
烛火比秋雾更深
漫步到天明

WAX

puberty's wax
hidden deep in the lock of memory
flame abandoned wine
passersby hurrying over the ruins
our hearts

our hearts
can go further than hate
night refuses tomorrow's reader
lit candlewax
dizzy as sky-altering
bells tolling over and over
the moment's only silence

the moment's only silence
is a naked flower garden
we're caught up in it for nothing
candle-flame deeper than autumn fog
strolling into dawn

关键词

我的影子很危险
这受雇于太阳的艺人
带来最后的知识
是空的

那是蛀虫工作的
黑暗属性
暴力的最小的孩子
空中的足音

关键词，我的影子
锤打着梦中之铁
踏着那节奏
一只孤狼走进

无人失败的黄昏
鹭鸶在水上书写
一生一天一个句子
结束

KEYWORD

my shadow's dangerous
this craftsman the sun hired
brings final knowledge
it's empty

that's the dark nature of
a moth's hungry work
smallest child of violence
footsteps in air

keyword my shadow
hammers dreamworld iron
stepping to that rhythm
a lone wolf walks into

dusk of no one's defeat
an egret writes on water
a life a day a sentence
ends

无 题

千百个窗户闪烁
这些预言者
在昨天与大海之间
哦迷途的欢乐

桥成为现实
跨越公共的光线
而涉及昨日玫瑰的
秘密旅行提供
一张纸一种困境

母亲的泪我的黎明

UNTITLED

windows glimmer by the thousand
these prophets
between yesterday and the sea
o that joy of losing the way

a bridge becomes reality
spanning the public's gleam
and the clandestine journey involving
yesterday's rose offers
a sheet of paper a dilemma

mother's tears my daybreak

远 景

海鸥，尖叫的梦
抗拒着信仰的天空
当草变成牛奶
风失去细节

若风是乡愁
道路就是其言说

在道路尽头
一只历史的走狗
扮装成夜
正向我逼近

夜的背后
有无边的粮食
伤心的爱人

THE LONG VIEW

seagulls, shriek dream
resisting skies of belief
when pasture becomes milk
wind loses detail

if wind is the longing for home
roads must be its speech

at the far end of the road
history's stooge
masquerades as night
and closes in on me

out back of night
it's boundless grain
heartbreak lover

边 境

风暴转向北方的未来
病人们的根在地下怒吼
太阳的螺旋桨
驱赶蜜蜂变成光芒
链条上的使者们
在那些招风耳里播种

被记住的河流
不再终结
被偷去了的声音
已成为边境

边境上没有希望
一本书
吞下一个翅膀
还有语言的坚冰中
赎罪的兄弟
你为此而斗争

BORDERS

storms turn toward the north's future
sick people's roots howl underground
a sun propeller
chases bees until they're rays of light
messengers in chains
sow seed in those ears long for the wind

remembered rivers
never end
stolen sound
becomes borders

borders allow no hope
a book
swallows a wing
and still in the hard ice of language
brothers redeem their crimes
you struggle on for this

借来方向

一条鱼的生活
充满了漏洞
流水的漏洞啊泡沫
那是我的言说

借来方向
醉汉穿过他的重重回声
而心是看家狗
永远朝向抒情的中心

行进中的音乐
被一次事故所粉碎
天空覆盖我们
感情生活的另一面

借来方向
候鸟挣脱了我的睡眠
闪电落入众人之杯
言者无罪

BORROWING A DIRECTION

a fish's life
is full of loopholes
streamwater's loopholes ah bubbles
that's my way of speaking

borrowing a direction
the drunk passes through his echoes layer by layer
but the heart's a watchdog
forever facing the lyric's essence

music driving forward
gets shattered in the accident
skies cover the other
side of our emotional life

borrowing a direction
migratory birds break out of my sleep
lightning strikes everyone's cup
the speaker's innocent

新 年

怀抱花朵的孩子走向新年
为黑暗文身的指挥啊
在倾听那最短促的停顿

快把狮子关进音乐的牢笼
快让石头佯装成隐士
在平行之夜移动

谁是客人？当所有的日子
倾巢而出在路上飞行
失败之书博大精深

每一刻都是捷径
我得以穿过东方的意义
回家，关上死亡之门

NEW YEAR

a child carrying flowers walks toward the new year
a conductor tattooing darkness
listens to the shortest pause

hurry a lion into the cage of music
hurry stone to masquerade as a recluse
moving in parallel nights

who's the visitor? when the days all
tip from nests and fly down roads
the book of failure grows boundless and deep

each moment a shortcut
I follow it through the meaning of the East
returning home, closing death's door

无 题

醒来是自由
那星辰之间的矛盾

门在抵抗岁月
丝绸卷走了叫喊
我是被你否认的身分
从心里关掉的灯

这脆弱的时刻
敌对的岸
风折叠所有的消息
记忆变成了主人

哦陈酒
因表达而变色
煤会遇见必然的矿灯
火不能为火作证

UNTITLED

in waking there is freedom
that contradiction among stars

doors resisting the years
silk carried screams away
I'm the identity you deny
lamp switched off in the heart

this fragile moment
hostile shores
wind folds up all the news
memory's become master

o vintage wine
changing color for clear expression
coal meets the miner's inevitable lamp
fire cannot bear witness to fire

冬之旅

谁在虚无上打字
太多的故事
是十二块石头
击中表盘
是十二只天鹅
飞离冬天

而夜里的舌头
描述着光线
盲目的钟
为缺席者呼喊

进入房间
你看见那个丑角
在进入冬天时
留下的火焰

WINTER TRAVELS

who's typing on the void
too many stories
they're twelve stones
hitting the clockface
twelve swans
flying out of winter

tongues in the night
describe gleams of light
blind bells
cry out for someone absent

entering the room
you see that jester's
entered winter
leaving behind flame

否 认

蒙面的纪念日
是一盏灯笼
收割从夜开始
到永恒

从死者的眼里
采摘棉花
冬天索回记忆
纺出十年长的风

日子成为路标
风叩响重音之门
果园没有历史
梦里没有医生

逃离纪念日
我呼吸并否认

deny

that a veiled anniversary
is a lantern
harvest begins at night
keeps on into forever

plucking cotton
from the eyes of the dead
winter demands memory's return
spinning out a decade-long wind

days become road signs
wind knocks at the gate of accented sounds
orchards have no history
dreams have no doctors

fleeing the anniversary
I breathe and deny

休 息

你终于到达
云朵停靠的星期天

休息，正如谎言
必须小心有人窥看

它在键盘上弹奏
白昼与黑夜

弹奏明天
那幸福的链条

死者挣脱了影子
锁住天空

REST

you finally arrive
at the sunday where clouds moor

rest, just like a lie
make sure no one's watching

it's performing on a keyboard
days white and nights black

performing tomorrow
that chain of happiness

the dead broke free of shadow
and locked up the sky

工 作

与它的影子竞赛
鸟变成了回声

并非偶然，你
在风暴中选择职业
是飞艇里的词
古老的记忆中的
刺

开窗的母亲
象旧书里的主人公
展开秋天的折扇
如此耀眼

你这不肖之子
用白云擦洗玻璃
擦洗玻璃中的自己

WORK

competing with its shadow
a bird becomes echo

not unexpectedly, you
choosing a profession in the storm
are the word inside zeppelins
ancient memory's
thorn

mother opening windows
like some hero in an old book
spreads autumn's fan open
dazzling the eyes

you unfilial son
wiping glass clean with white cloud
wiping the self in glass clean

旅 行

那影子在饮水
那笑声模仿
撑开黎明的光线的
崩溃方式

带着书去旅行
书因旅行获得年龄
因旅行而匿名
那深入布景的马
回首

你刚好到达
那人出生的地方

鱼从水下看城市
水下有新鲜的诱饵
令人难堪的锚

JOURNEY

that shadow's drinking water
laughter mimics
the dawn-opening gleam's
collapsing ways

you set out on a journey with books
books age because of journeys
hide their names because of journeys
that horse deep in the stage scenery
turns its head

you've just arrived
at that person's birthplace

fish watch the city from underwater
among fresh bait underwater
there's an embarrassing anchor

Index

of titles and first lines in English
(first lines are in italics)